Original title:
Verses in Vaults

Copyright © 2024 Creative Arts Management OÜ
All rights reserved.

Author: Thor Castlebury
ISBN HARDBACK: 978-9916-88-060-9
ISBN PAPERBACK: 978-9916-88-061-6

Beneath the Cloistered Roof

In shadows deep, where whispers hide,
Ancient stones by time abide.
A quiet grace, a sacred space,
Secrets linger, like soft lace.

The light that slips through weathered beams,
Casts dancing patterns, golden dreams.
Upon the walls where stories dwell,
Beneath the roof, all hearts can tell.

Chorus of the Sealed Writings

In dusty tomes, the voices wait,
Tales of love, and of fate.
Ink spills truths, both harsh and sweet,
In silence, they await the meet.

Each page a song, the echoes rise,
From hidden depths to open skies.
Words entwined in sacred dance,
Calling forth a timeless chance.

The Crypt's Unheard Melodies

Within the crypt, the stillness grows,
A symphony that no one knows.
Each breath of dust, a note of grace,
In shadows deep, they find their place.

Forgotten tunes in stone embrace,
Hushed vibrations of time and space.
Resonating in the heart's own beat,
Melodies of loss, bittersweet.

Guardians of the Silent Words

The silent guards, they watch the tome,
In secret chambers, they find home.
With watchful eyes, their meaning spans,
The timeless truth in ancient plans.

They bind the tales that time forgot,
In whispered tones, the truths they wrought.
Through ages past their wisdom flows,
Guardians still, as knowledge grows.

Quiet Echoes from Hidden Vaults

In the depths where whispers stay,
Shadows dance in soft ballet.
Memories linger, gently spun,
Fleeting shadows, lost but won.

Time wears thin on fragile pages,
Secrets hid in ancient cages.
Silent sighs of stories told,
Echoes weaving threads of gold.

Tapestries of Secluded Melodies

In corners where the silence hums,
Softly play the unseen drums.
Notes entwine in subtle grace,
Carving out a sacred space.

Colors blend in vibrant hue,
Filling voids with thoughts anew.
Each thread a tale, a voice, a dream,
A symphony, a quiet stream.

Silent Celebrations of the Past

In stillness, voices rise in cheer,
Honoring those who once were near.
Candles flicker with a warm embrace,
Memories etched, time won't erase.

A gentle toast to fleeting years,
Bathed in laughter, softened fears.
With every heartbeat, life is spun,
Acknowledged joys of battles won.

Burdened Stories in Crated Odysseys

Beneath the weight of time and scars,
Stories hide like distant stars.
Each crate a world of hopes and dreams,
Wrapped in silence, frayed at seams.

As journeys whisper through the night,
Lessons learned in faded light.
Threads of fate a tapestry,
Carved in realms we long to see.

Veiled Elegies of the Forgotten

In shadows cast by faded light,
Whispers echo from the night.
Names long lost, yet still they tread,
In silence where their dreams are wed.

Forgotten songs of heart's lament,
In every sigh, a life well-spent.
Memories draped like fragile lace,
Entwined in time, a silent grace.

Voices linger on the wind,
Tales of love that would not end.
Each heartbeat carries tales untold,
A history, both dark and bold.

Among the graves where lilies weep,
Lay secrets that the ancients keep.
Veils of sorrow, woven tight,
In elegies that haunt the night.

The Untold Symphony

Notes like butterflies take flight,
Dancing softly in the night.
A melody that winds its way,
Through hidden paths that dreams display.

Echoes of a soul long gone,
Resonating like a song.
Harmonies in shadows blend,
Where beginnings meet the end.

The grand refrain of what's not said,
In every tear, a dream is fed.
Moments caught in timeless grace,
In silence, find their rightful place.

Unseen whispers float on air,
Drawn from depths of dark despair.
Yet in chaos, there's a tune,
A symphony beneath the moon.

Harbored Dreams in Confidential Corners

In corners where the shadows play,
Dreams are cradled, kept at bay.
Whispers follow like a ghost,
In gentle sighs, we hold them close.

Hidden hopes that softly gleam,
Nestled in the heart's warm beam.
Confidential thoughts take flight,
On wings of solace through the night.

Here, amidst the life's swirling dance,
We find refuge, given chance.
Nestled deep within the mind,
A sanctuary, rare to find.

Out of sight but never lost,
These harbored dreams, we bear the cost.
In moments cherished, they reside,
Our secrets kept, our hearts their guide.

Secrets Written in Midnight Ink

By candle's light, I write the truth,
In midnight ink, the dreams of youth.
Each stroke a story, dark and deep,
In fragile whispers, secrets keep.

The paper thirsts for tales untold,
Ink runs freely, bold and cold.
Hidden within every line,
Lies a world, a heart divine.

Shadows dance as words emerge,
In quiet corners, feelings surge.
With every drop, a memory flows,
In midnight ink, our sorrow grows.

Faded pages hold our fears,
Ink-stained visions through the years.
But in the dark, the heart can sing,
Of all the secrets midnight brings.

Cadences of the Concealed

Whispers float on gentle air,
Secrets held with tender care.
Notes resound in shadows deep,
Echoes of what dreams can keep.

Fingers trace the hidden marks,
A symphony of quiet sparks.
Every silence holds a song,
In the dark where thoughts belong.

In the stillness, masks unveil,
Truths emerge, they will not fail.
Hear the rhythms of the night,
Life's pure pulse, a soft twilight.

With each breath, the heart perceives,
In the silence, hope retrieves.
Cadences of the heart unfold,
Stories subtle, yet untold.

Tales Carved in Stone

Ancient rocks with stories lie,
Whispers of a time gone by.
Chiseled dreams, a silent plea,
Nature's voice, a reverie.

Weathered surface, wisdom speaks,
In the stillness, history peaks.
With every contour, life's embrace,
Moments trapped in their own space.

Rivers flow and winds have blown,
Yet the tales remain alone.
Time will fade but stones will stand,
Guardians of both sea and land.

Eternal echoes, soft and vast,
Memories of ages past.
In the rock, our truths are sown,
In their silence, life is grown.

Harmony in Encrypted Expressions

Symbols woven, thoughts concealed,
Meaning found, yet unpeeled.
Layers deep with colors bright,
Harmony in hidden light.

Lines entwined with rhythm's grace,
Secrets dance in each embrace.
Voices rise in silent streams,
Echoing our hidden dreams.

Truth contained in lines we trace,
Mystery within each face.
Understanding wrapped in sound,
In the silence, truth is found.

Expressions forged through time and space,
In the quiet, we find our place.
Harmony soft, like a breeze,
Encrypted voices seek to please.

The Vision of Silent Archives

In the shadows, stories curl,
Timeless tales begin to unfurl.
Silent records, wisdom's art,
In the still, the journeys start.

Pages whisper of the past,
Moments caught that forever last.
Unseen glimpses of the wise,
In the calm, a world inside.

Feel the echoes of the pens,
Silent voices, ancient friends.
The archives hold what time can't steal,
Capturing what we often feel.

With each leaf, new visions rise,
In the silence, truth implies.
The archives keep our stories clear,
In their embrace, we feel them near.

Threads Woven in Silence

In the quiet corners, secrets sway,
Gentle whispers thread the night away.
Embroidered dreams in shadows lie,
Every stitch a story, an unheeded sigh.

Fingers dance upon the loom,
Weaving tales in the silent room.
Colors fade but truth remains,
In woven silence, life gains chains.

Threads of hope and threads of fear,
Every fiber holds a tear.
Through the fabric, spirits glide,
In this tapestry, we all abide.

Softly pulling at the seams,
Fragile patterns form our dreams.
In silence, meanings intertwine,
Threads woven deep, forever entwine.

Fragments from the Labyrinth

In twisted paths, where shadows blend,
Whispers echo, the maze shall bend.
Each corner turned, a tale unfolds,
A flicker of truth in secrets told.

A fleeting moment, a ghost of time,
Bittersweet rhythms, a silent rhyme.
Through intricate turns, we search and find,
Fragments of stories left behind.

In the heart of the maze, we chase the light,
Seeking redemption from endless night.
Yet every choice, a blurred divide,
In labyrinth's grasp, we must confide.

Gather the pieces, mend the whole,
Each fragment whispers to the soul.
For in the twists, the journey's grace,
Fragments remind us of our place.

Whispers from the Worn Pages

Ancient tomes with covers frayed,
Hold the whispers of those who've stayed.
Every line a touch of grace,
Stories linger in this space.

Dusty words that softly speak,
In their silence, truths we seek.
Echoes of laughter, shadows of pain,
Worn pages hide the unclaimed gain.

In the margins, dreams reside,
Thoughts unraveled, where hopes collide.
Turn the pages, let history flow,
In whispers of wisdom, let us grow.

With every glimpse of ink and lore,
A universe waits to explore.
Through worn pages, life engages,
In timeless whispers of the ages.

Concealed Chronicles of Time

Beneath the surface, timelines lie,
Hidden chapters that never die.
Concealed secrets in every glance,
Chronicles waiting for a chance.

Silent clocks tick away the hours,
Each moment blooms like hidden flowers.
Time's embrace, a fleeting touch,
In concealed stories, we learn so much.

Woven deep in the fabric of days,
Chronicles echo in myriad ways.
Unlock the vault, reveal the rhyme,
In the shadows of concealed time.

Whispered echoes of lives once lived,
In every choice, what we've forgiven.
Through the veils, we dare to dream,
Concealed chronicles, a flowing stream.

Whispers in the Citadel

In shadows deep, the echoes sing,
Ancient stones, their secrets cling.
Above the walls, the moonlight glows,
Whispers of time, in silence flow.

Guardians watch, with eyes so wise,
Tales of yore beneath the skies.
A breeze unravels the woven fates,
Through narrow halls and gilded gates.

Each fluttered page, a breath of lore,
In every crack, the past implores.
Heroes lost, and battles brave,
In whispered tones, our souls they save.

Within the heart, the stories weave,
In dreams of night, we still believe.
The citadel holds what time won't claim,
In mystic realms, we stake our name.

Chambered Thoughts of the Ages

In chambers dark, where silence reigns,
Thoughts converge, free from the chains.
Echoes linger, from far-off days,
In whispered tones, the mind obeys.

Each scroll unrolls, a treasure found,
In every note, the past is bound.
Fragments of dreams, like dust in light,
Awakening souls from endless night.

Eyes of sages gaze through time,
In every word, a subtle rhyme.
The tales of old, in layers unfold,
Every heartbeat, a story told.

In this abode, where echoes meet,
Wisdom flows, bittersweet.
Chambered thoughts, a sacred space,
In every glance, we find our place.

The Vault of Elusive Verses

In hidden vaults, soft verses lie,
Crafted words that seem to fly.
Each syllable, a fleeting glance,
In twilight's grip, they weave and dance.

Guarded tightly, these phrases rare,
Whispers wrapped in fragrant air.
A chorus of dreams beneath the sun,
Elusive thoughts, they weigh a ton.

Yet in their depths, the heart will sing,
Of distant shores and a promising spring.
Through countless trials, we will roam,
In every verse, we find our home.

Open the doors, let them cascade,
In vibrant hues, our fears evade.
The vault shall gleam, when penned with grace,
Elusive verses, our timeless embrace.

Stanzas Encased in Silence

In shadows deep, a whisper dwells,
Unspoken thoughts in secret spells.
The hush of night, a calm embrace,
Where echoes linger, time slows its pace.

Beneath the moon, soft dreams take flight,
Entwined in silence, lost from sight.
A tapestry of muted sighs,
In quietude, their beauty lies.

Each breath a pause, a moment still,
Captured thoughts that time cannot kill.
In solitude, the heart may sing,
Of stanzas veiled, the peace they bring.

Yet in the void, a spark ignites,
A tale unfolds under starlit nights.
Awakened dreams in silence rise,
In whispered words, the spirit flies.

The Canvases of Enigma

On azure skies, the colors blend,
Painting mysteries that never end.
Brushstrokes whisper secrets bold,
In every hue, a story told.

Shapes emerge from shadows low,
In every corner, a tale to show.
The artist's heart, an open door,
Inviting all to seek for more.

With every frame, a puzzle waits,
Each gaze unravels hidden fates.
Entangled truths and veiled design,
In the gallery of the divine.

Eclipsed in thought, the mind takes flight,
With questions born from pure delight.
The enigma wraps its tender arms,
In silent awe, its mystery charms.

Tunes of Tattered Pages

Old books whisper, secrets kept,
In dusty corners where dreams have slept.
Notes of history, a fragile sound,
In every page, lost tales are found.

The melody of ink and time,
Eloquent words in rhythm and rhyme.
Through crinkled leaves, the past will cry,
In tunes of wisdom, we learn to fly.

Chapters echo, lessons learned,
Flickering flames from passion burned.
Each turn a song, each pause a dance,
In ancient verses, we take a chance.

A serenade of stories told,
In fragile tomes, a treasure of gold.
With every note, the heart engages,
To read the world through tattered pages.

Chants From the Cloistered Corners

In hallowed halls where shadows play,
Soft chants arise at the end of day.
Echoes of prayer, a sacred sound,
In cloistered corners, peace is found.

Each whispered hope, a gentle plea,
Carried on waves of tranquility.
The heartbeats blend, a soft refrain,
Uniting souls in joy and pain.

From hidden nooks, the voices soar,
In unity, they forever implore.
The light of faith through silent tears,
Resounding hope throughout the years.

In the stillness, the spirits sigh,
Hearts open wide, the world complies.
From cloistered corners, a sacred chance,
To find redemption in this dance.

The Silent Song of the Ancients

In the forest deep, whispers call,
Echoes of ages, lost to the thrall.
Trees stand silent, guardians of lore,
Holding the secrets of those before.

Moonlit shadows dance on the ground,
Ancient echoes in the silence found.
Mysteries linger in the cool night air,
A haunting melody, everywhere.

With every breeze, a memory stirs,
The language of time, in whispers and purrs.
Starlit paths guide the way across,
To the lost rhythms where dreams are tossed.

Feel the heartbeat of the olden past,
In every rustle, a spell is cast.
The silent song of the ancients endures,
In the heart of the wild, its magic lures.

Reflections in Timeless Corners

Beneath the arch of ancient stone,
Footsteps echo, yet we're alone.
Mirrors hold the tales of yore,
Reflections beckon us to explore.

Through weathered doors, a world unfolds,
Forgotten stories, lovingly told.
Time stands still in these sacred halls,
Whispers of beauty as twilight calls.

In every shadow, in every frame,
Lies a flicker of a childhood game.
A dance of moments, so bittersweet,
Lives intertwined in the echoes we meet.

Let the quiet guide us, soft and slow,
To the timeless corners where memories glow.
In the heart's gallery, we find our place,
In reflections hidden, we embrace grace.

Hidden Harmonies

In the secret glen where wildflowers bloom,
Nature's melody dispels the gloom.
Notes of laughter twirl in the breeze,
Hidden harmonies rise with such ease.

Butterflies flutter to an unseen song,
Wings whisper tales of where they belong.
The brook hums softly, a soothing rhyme,
In every ripple, the pulse of time.

Moonbeams waltz on the still, cool lake,
While crickets join in, no sound to break.
Together they weave a tapestry bright,
Of hidden harmonies that dance in the night.

Listen closely, let your heart be free,
To the symphony sung by earth and tree.
In the quiet moments, let joy ascend,
For in hidden harmonies, we find a friend.

Buried Narratives

In the dusty tomes, stories sleep,
Buried narratives, secrets they keep.
Pages worn thin from decades of sighs,
Whispers of dreams beneath ancient skies.

Tales of love lost, and battles fought,
Lessons forgotten, yet never caught.
Each word a treasure, a portal to see,
The lives that lived and the hearts that were free.

In quiet corners of dim-lit rooms,
Echoes of laughter blend with the gloom.
Every letter a bridge to the past,
In buried narratives, shadows are cast.

Flowing ink tells of journeys afar,
Of midnight wishes and wishes on stars.
Delve into histories, let curiosity reign,
For buried narratives long to be gained.

Shadows of the Silent Archive

In the corner where whispers fade,
Dust clings tight like secrets laid.
Faded pages, stories lost,
Dreams imprisoned, at what cost?

Cobwebs stretch in twilight's grace,
Time stands still in this still place.
Echoes linger, soft and old,
Forgotten tales yet to be told.

Each shadow speaks in muted tones,
Carrying whispers, ancient moans.
A library where silence reigns,
Guarding truths and hidden pains.

With cautious steps, we delve within,
Seeking light where darkness begins.
In the shadows, knowledge sleeps,
Awaiting those who dare to peep.

Relics of the Unspoken

Beneath the layers of dust and years,
Lie dreams wrapped in uncried tears.
Objects whisper from years gone by,
Inviting hearts to wonder why.

Each relic holds a tale of yore,
Fragments of lives that lived before.
Echoes trapped in wooden frames,
Calling softly, bearing names.

Silence reigns on this hallowed ground,
As history breathes without a sound.
In corners dim, the memories wane,
Yet curiosity cannot remain.

We tread lightly on this sacred space,
Unveiling stories that time can't erase.
With each discovery, we unlock the past,
Building bridges with shadows cast.

Inked Memories in Dusty Corners

Pages yellowed, ink fading fast,
Captured moments from a distant past.
In dusty corners, stories hide,
Each line a journey, a cherished guide.

Quills danced lightly on fragile sheets,
As dreams flowed freely in rhythmic beats.
Whispers penned in heart's own ink,
Waiting patiently for us to think.

Ink blots tell of passions bright,
Echoing laughter in the pale moonlight.
Lost loves, regrets, and joyful tears,
Imprinted deeply, with passing years.

In these corners of written grace,
We find our souls in time and space.
Inked memories, both bitter and sweet,
Unraveling tales at our own heartbeat.

The Attic of Unwritten Stories

High above with a gentle creak,
An attic's hush, where no one speaks.
Dusty beams hold unturned dreams,
In silence, life unfolds in seams.

Boxes stacked from floor to eave,
Each one holds what we believe.
With every glance, a memory calls,
Bringing life to these four walls.

Pages blank, yet filled with hope,
Starlit thoughts as we learn to cope.
Lost words yearn for a voice to say,
In quietude, they wait to play.

In this attic, the heart takes flight,
Unwritten stories dance in the light.
With pen in hand, we rise and roam,
Turning whispers into a home.

The Vault of Echoing Dreams

In the quiet night, whispers thread,
Through the corridors of thoughts unsaid.
Shadows dance where hopes collide,
In the vault where memories abide.

Fleeting glances of a bygone time,
Chasing echoes that softly chime.
Fragments of laughter, shadows of light,
In this sacred space, dreams take flight.

Ancient secrets wrapped in mist,
In every heartbeat, a fragile twist.
The vault holds stories, tales untold,
In whispers of silver, and glimmers of gold.

Awake the dreams that softly sigh,
As stars blink softly in the sky.
The vault invites those who dare,
To wander through the echoing air.

Shadows Cast by Ink.

In the dim-lit room, shadows play,
Ink spills tales that fade away.
Fingers dance on pages torn,
While whispers of history are gently born.

Underneath the scribbles of fate,
Lies a world we contemplate.
Characters leap from every line,
In the ink, their souls intertwine.

Echoes linger, stories grow,
In shadows cast, we seek to know.
Every stroke a flight of dreams,
In the darkness, light softly gleams.

Beneath the surface, secrets gleam,
In the quiet, we find our theme.
Ink and paper, a sacred bond,
In the shadows, the heart responds.

Echoes of Hidden Chambers

In chambers deep, where echoes dwell,
Whispers in the silence tell.
Secrets linger in shadows deep,
In hidden corners, memories sleep.

Faded portraits on the wall,
Recalling moments, both grand and small.
Echoes weave a tapestry strong,
Of love, of loss, a haunting song.

Each chamber holds a story vast,
Of laughter, sorrows, memories cast.
In the stillness, shadows sway,
In hidden chambers, dreams replay.

Unlock the door and step inside,
Let the echoes be your guide.
In every sigh, a tale unfolds,
In hidden chambers, secrets hold.

Whispers Behind Forgotten Doors

Behind closed doors, whispers creep,
In shadows where the memories seep.
Forgotten tales linger near,
In silence, they beckon, soft and clear.

Dust gathers on the ancient frame,
Yet the whispers call out by name.
Every crack carries a sigh,
Of moments lost that still imply.

Pale light flickers, dreams awake,
In the quiet, hearts often break.
Behind the doors, the past resides,
In whispers where the lost bide.

Step softly through the hidden past,
Where echoes of longing forever last.
In whispers low, the stories soar,
Behind forgotten doors, forevermore.

Echoing Through Thick Stone

In halls where whispers die,
The echoes softly roam,
Carried through the years,
In this forgotten home.

Silence wraps the corners,
As shadows creep and wane,
Each footstep tells a story,
Of love and lingering pain.

Beneath the weighty arches,
Time slows its swift embrace,
While memories like phantoms,
Leave their indelible trace.

In every crack and crevice,
Lies a tale yet to be told,
Of laughter, tears, and heartbeats,
Entwined in stone so bold.

The Poetry of Concealed Spaces

Behind the closed doors lie,
Whispers of hidden dreams,
Fragments of forgotten tales,
Woven in silent seams.

A nook in the olden wood,
Holds secrets bittersweet,
Where time's rhythm breathes softly,
In corners where shadows meet.

The silence holds a canvas,
For thoughts unspoken, raw,
In the heart of concealed spaces,
Life's beauty is in flaw.

With every gentle rustle,
A story starts to bloom,
In quietude, they flourish,
Finding voice in shadowed rooms.

Unseen Verses in Candlelight

Flickering flames reveal,
The stories yet untold,
In the glow of candlelight,
Mysteries unfold.

Dancing shadows play along,
The walls that know the night,
Whispers weave through the darkness,
In the embrace of light.

Each drip of wax a heartbeat,
Time captured in its fall,
As verses twist in silence,
Echoing through the hall.

In this moment suspended,
Thoughts twine like the smoke,
Unseen yet palpable,
In poetry that evokes.

The Language of Sealed Promises

Beneath the rusted surface,
Lies a promise yet to bloom,
In words sealed by hesitation,
Waiting to fill the room.

Each glance holds a story,
Of what could have been said,
In the quiet of longing,
Where the heart gently bled.

The silence is a canvas,
Painted with hope's soft sighs,
A language of unspoken,
Written in hushed goodbyes.

In the trust of whispered vows,
Lie treasures yet unseen,
Sealed in endless patience,
Cradled in spaces between.

Pages Beyond the Grave

In shadows deep where whispers wane,
The stories dwell of joy and pain.
Forgotten tales in silence breathe,
Their echoes linger, hearts believe.

Each flickered flame, a soul's delight,
Unfolds a journey, lost from sight.
Through dusty tomes, the past we find,
A tapestry of love unkind.

While parchment's scent reveals the truth,
We chase the trails of fleeting youth.
In every line, a life once told,
Their words transform to hues of gold.

So here we stand, with hearts aglow,
In pages turned, the secrets flow.
Beyond the grave, through time we dare,
To seek the lives that linger there.

Unraveled Scrolls of Time

Beneath the stars, the whispers play,
Unraveled scrolls from yesterday.
In ink and parchment, dreams take flight,
As shadows dance within the night.

Each curve and line, a story bears,
Of ancient hearts and whispered cares.
Through epochs vast, their voices strain,
To guide us through the joy and pain.

The moments freeze in time's embrace,
Emotions caught, a fleeting trace.
We uncover paths of fate entwined,
In every page, our hearts aligned.

So let us read the tales once spun,
In timeless echoes, we're all one.
With every scroll, the past we hold,
In threads of time, the memories gold.

The Cryptic Lyric

In whispers soft, the echoes blend,
A cryptic tune that twists and bends.
With hidden meanings tucked away,
These lyrics haunt the light of day.

In every word, a secret glows,
A riddle wrapped in lyrical prose.
The heart must listen, hear the call,
For truth resides where shadows fall.

Each note cascades like rain on stone,
Revealing paths we walk alone.
In melodies, the past unfolds,
Through cryptic words, the heart consoled.

So delve into this world profound,
Where hidden songs of time abound.
The cryptic lyric sings its tune,
A guiding light beneath the moon.

Underneath the Weaving Spire

Beneath the arch where dreams converge,
A weaver's hand begins to surge.
With threads of fate, the patterns lie,
In every stitch, a whispered sigh.

In colors bright and hues of fate,
The tapestry of love and hate.
Each woven tale, a life embraced,
In shadows cast, our dreams interlaced.

The spire looms, a watchful guide,
Through tangled paths where secrets hide.
For every yarn, a story streams,
In woven whispers, hope redeems.

So let us tread with care and grace,
Underneath the spire's embrace.
Together we will weave our thread,
In fabric rich with dreams long fed.

Fragments of the Forgotten

Whispers echo in the night,
Lost stories fade from side to side.
Dusty pages, fragile light,
In shadows where the past resides.

Ghosts of laughter filled the air,
Memories drifting, out of reach.
Silent cries of fleeting care,
In the ruins of what we teach.

Echoes linger, yearning still,
Fragments pieced from shattered time.
Hearts once heavy, now are thrill,
Finding solace in the rhyme.

Each old token, a tapestry,
Woven tight with threads of grace.
In the end, what's left of me,
Are the shadows that we embrace.

The Secret Symphony of Seclusion

In quiet corners, secrets dwell,
Unseen dances sway in light.
Silken notes that softly swell,
In the stillness of the night.

A hidden tune, a whispered call,
Beats that pulse in hidden heart.
Melodies like silent thrall,
Binding souls that drift apart.

In solitude, a sound so sweet,
Fingers trace the air like lace.
Harmony in still retreat,
The rhythm finds its rightful place.

Each quiet moment held sublime,
Unfolds a world we dare not share.
In seclusion's embrace, we climb,
To find the music, always there.

Resonance of the Withheld

Voices trapped behind the veil,
Echoes shiver, soft and meek.
Words unspoken start to pale,
The silent truth we fear to seek.

In branches bare, a truth resides,
Fragrant whispers on the breeze.
Longing hearts that ache and bide,
To voice the love beneath the leaves.

A symphony of unmet dreams,
Each note stifled, held in pain.
In quietude, the spirit beams,
As untold stories seek the rain.

For what we hide can shine so bright,
When released from a cautious throat.
Beyond the shadows of the night,
Resounding echoes bid us float.

Notes Trapped in Dungeons

In crumbling depths, the echoes sigh,
Notes confined in iron chains.
Beneath the stone, they dream to fly,
Yearning to break their silent pains.

Ghostly whispers, shadows cast,
Carried forth on rocky wings.
Each refrain too bold to last,
In longing silence, the heart sings.

Dusty scrolls with stories locked,
Hopes entwined in webs of time.
Melodies that fate has mocked,
Await the key—a secret rhyme.

If only light could touch the dark,
And minds could free what's held so tight.
In dungeons deep, ignite a spark,
To unleash notes into the night.

Chronicles of Unseen Ink

In shadows deep, the stories sleep,
Whispers penned where secrets keep.
Pages turn with silent grace,
Unseen ink, a hidden trace.

Memories float like gentle sighs,
Ink-stained dreams under darkened skies.
Every word, a fleeting ghost,
Chronicles of what we lost the most.

Ephemeral tales in twilight gleam,
Fleeting moments, a tender dream.
Each stroke tells of joy and pain,
Unseen ink, a soft refrain.

With careful hands, the truths unfurl,
In silent realms, our thoughts swirl.
The ink may fade, but hearts ignite,
Chronicles shine in the still of night.

Echoes from Within

In hollow halls, the echoes ring,
Voices lost, yet memories cling.
Whispers paint the walls with grace,
A dance of past in hidden space.

From silence deep, the thoughts take flight,
In shadows cast, they find their light.
A symphony of dreams and fears,
Echoes blend with fleeting years.

In every corner, soft sighs blend,
Stories shared, yet time won't mend.
The heart remembers, beats like drum,
Echoes from within, softly hum.

A gentle voice calls from the deep,
Awakening secrets we dare to keep.
In every echo, truths align,
Whispers linger, transcend the line.

The Tranquil Art of Concealment

Beneath the calm, the currents flow,
Softly shrouded, secrets grow.
In quiet light, the shadows weave,
The tranquil art, we often believe.

Like water still, reflections lie,
Hidden truths beneath the sky.
Softly spoken, each word a veil,
In the silence, we inhale.

The beauty lies in what remains,
In whispered thoughts, the heart refrains.
The art of keeping, a gentle hand,
Concealment's grace, an unseen strand.

In tranquil pools, the depths surprise,
With layered meaning, the spirit flies.
What's held within speaks loud and clear,
The art of concealment, a treasure dear.

Tones from the Enclosed Realm

In cloistered spaces, shadows play,
A symphony of hues at bay.
Echoed tones that softly call,
From the enclosed, we rise and fall.

Colors swirl in whispers low,
Gentle hands crafting the flow.
In every shade, a tale unfolds,
Tones from the realm, a journey bold.

The heartbeat thrums in tune with light,
Enclosed whispers, a dance of night.
With every brush, emotions bloom,
In tones alive, they dispel the gloom.

In the art of stillness, we find release,
Tones of solace, a sweet peace.
In every corner, stories gleam,
From the enclosed realm, we dare to dream.

Echoes from Encrypted Echoes

Whispers dance in shadowed halls,
Secrets shared where silence calls.
Voices lost in cryptic tone,
Vows of trust that lie alone.

Memories pulse like fleeting light,
Guiding souls through endless night.
Echoes weave a fragile thread,
Binding hearts where fears once led.

In the maze of thoughts concealed,
Truths arise, once unrevealed.
Softly speaking through the dark,
Hope ignites a quiet spark.

Yet the echoes softly fade,
Leaving shadows, dreams betrayed.
Still, they linger in the mind,
Promises of life entwined.

Forgotten Lines in the Gloom

In whispered tones where shadows creep,
Secrets held that time won't keep.
Lines once penned, now lost in haze,
Fragments of forgotten days.

Through the fog, a flickered spark,
Guides the dreams that haunt the dark.
Silent cries in rusted rooms,
Breath of life in silent glooms.

Pages yellowed, ink erased,
Stories told but long misplaced.
Memories fade, yet still they yearn,
For the light of hearts that burn.

In the night where echoes sigh,
Lines re-write, they never die.
Though the gloom may veil their sight,
Hope will rise and claim the night.

Inked Dreams in Safe Havens

In the stillness, dreams take flight,
Inked with shadows, kissed by light.
Sketched in hearts, the dreams do dwell,
In safe havens, they weave their spell.

Silent wishes float like seeds,
Carried forth on whispered needs.
In the gardens of the mind,
Every vision, intertwined.

Colors bright on canvas bare,
Brush of hope in tender care.
In each stroke, a story grows,
In dark places, courage flows.

Yet the ink may sometimes fade,
Leaving whispers in its shade.
But deep within, those dreams survive,
In safe havens, they revive.

The Chronicles of Cavernous Dreams

Deep within the earth we roam,
Caverns dark, a twisted home.
Chronicles of night unfold,
Tales of warmth in pockets cold.

Echoes linger in the air,
Silent secrets, shadows stare.
Stories carved in rugged stone,
Whispered fears we call our own.

In the depths, where light is rare,
Hope ignites with gentle flare.
Ventures lead us to explore,
Caverns hide forevermore.

Each heartbeat soft, a daring quest,
Threads of fate put to the test.
In our dreams, these tales reside,
Chronicles that won't subside.

Requiem of the Object Known

In shadows cast by silent stone,
The whispers of what once was shown.
A tale of dust, a fleeting breath,
An elegy of quiet death.

Memories adorn the weathered frame,
Fading softly, none remains the same.
The weight of time, an anchor's hold,
In stories left, and truths untold.

Each fracture speaks of moments lost,
In reverie, we count the cost.
The heart of history, slow and deep,
In every echo, secrets keep.

Thus we honor, in gentle sighs,
The relics born beneath the skies.
In reverence, we lay them bare,
A requiem, for those who care.

Tapestry of Hidden Chronicles

Threads of gold interlace in dreams,
Weaving tales, or so it seems.
In quiet corners, stories hide,
Buried deep, where shadows bide.

Each stitch a moment, every hue,
A silent witness to the true.
Beneath the surface, colors blend,
A dance of spirits, heartbeats mend.

In labyrinths of thought, we roam,
Mapping paths we call our home.
The fabric speaks, a gentle guide,
Unraveling what we hold inside.

With every knot, a tale unfolds,
Secrets shared, and dreams retold.
In this tapestry, we intertwine,
Echoes of love, in each design.

Chamber of the Unexpressed

In silence thick, the shadows dwell,
A chamber where the stories swell.
Unuttered words and thoughts confined,
In secret vaults, the heart aligned.

Fractured ink upon the page,
An inner storm, a silent rage.
Lost whispers linger in the air,
In this small space, we learn to bear.

Emotions trapped, like birds in cage,
Yearning for a voice, a stage.
Each tear unshed, a tale unseen,
In muted echoes, we convene.

Unlock the door, let chaos free,
Express what's hidden, let it be.
In this chamber, we seek to find,
The power dwelling in the mind.

The Echoing Heart of Antiquity

Beneath the ruins, whispers fade,
Carved in stone, the dreams we made.
Old echoes dance on ancient ground,
In every crevice, shadows sound.

Time wears lightly on cracked skin,
Each pulse a story hidden within.
In history's breath, we hear a call,
A promise that transcends us all.

The heart of ages, strong and vast,
Preserving those who dared to last.
In every echo, wisdom sings,
Tales of mortals, of kings and things.

With every heartbeat, time does weave,
A tapestry of what we believe.
In antiquity's arms, we remain,
Holding fast through joy and pain.

Secrets Beneath the Dust

Whispers linger on the ground,
Memories lost, yet still profound.
Footprints trace where souls have walked,
In the silence, they have talked.

Beneath the layers, stories sleep,
Ancient secrets we long to keep.
Dusty tomes and faded dreams,
Lurking close, or so it seems.

Echoes of a distant past,
Time reveals what's meant to last.
In the shadows, truths emerge,
Waiting for a voice to urge.

With every breath, we sift through days,
Finding light in dusty ways.
Secrets woven, deep in trust,
A gentle touch, beneath the dust.

Melodies of the Enclosed

In the chambers, echoes play,
Softened notes in bright array.
Voices sing of hopes and fears,
Carried softly through the years.

The walls respond with tender sighs,
Harmonies that never die.
Strains of love and loss entwine,
A symphony, divine design.

Within the heart, the rhythm beats,
Melodies that time repeats.
In this space, so rich and lured,
Harmony and peace ensured.

Life enclosed, yet still so wide,
Melodies that gently guide.
Through the air, we find our way,
In the music, we shall stay.

Shadows Within Stony Walls

Beneath the stone, shadows creep,
Secrets that the walls do keep.
Every crack conceals a tale,
In silence, echoes thin and pale.

Light and dark in dance entwined,
Mysteries of the heart defined.
Whispers roam through cobblestone,
In the shadows, I am known.

Time has etched its quiet grace,
In this solemn, sacred space.
With every step, the stony breath,
A reminder of life and death.

Shadows wrap with gentle hold,
Warm and weary, shy yet bold.
Finding solace where we fall,
In the shadows, we embrace all.

Lyrical Lockboxes

Among the shelves, the boxes wait,
Each one holds a verse of fate.
Lyrical treasures softly sigh,
Nestled close, they dare to fly.

In the corners, secrets sleep,
Guarded dreams we long to keep.
Open gently, hearts will race,
Finding magic in this space.

Worn and weathered, tales unfold,
In these boxes, stories told.
Bound in ribbon, sealed with care,
Whispers caught in stillness there.

Each lockbox holds a piece of time,
Rhythms bound in every rhyme.
In the silence, voices rise,
Lyrical truths, our spirits prize.

Ballads of the Unobtrusive

In corners where shadows creep,
Soft whispers of secrets keep.
Gentle echoes of the night,
Fleeting thoughts take gentle flight.

Winds carry tales, old and wise,
Beneath the vast and quiet skies.
Unsung songs, a subtle call,
Embraced by trees that rise and fall.

Lurking dreams in shadows hide,
In silence, they will always bide.
The unseen paths we rarely tread,
Hold countless stories left unsaid.

Through shadows deep, we wander slow,
Where only the brave dare to go.
In unobtrusive, quiet grace,
We find our home in time and space.

Rhyme Trapped in the Dark

In silence thick, a heartbeat pounds,
Lost in echoes, no hope surrounds.
A whisper trapped in shadows gray,
Yearning for the light of day.

Words collide like stars in void,
In darkness forged, their hearts avoided.
Each verse a ghost, a haunting sigh,
That flickers like a firefly.

But still they dance in twilight's breath,
A gentle fight against the death.
In shadowed corners, tunes will stir,
With melodies that softly blur.

Through every line, despair may cling,
Yet from the dark, the heart will spring.
For trapped in rhyme, the spirit cries,
And from the dark, a song will rise.

Grace Among the Dusty Tomes

In silent halls where whispers dwell,
Old stories weave their magic spell.
Dust settles on forgotten dreams,
Where knowledge fades and sunlight beams.

Among the shelves, the shadows roam,
In ancient thoughts, we find our home.
Each spine worn with history's brush,
In pages filled, the voices hush.

With gentle hands, we turn the leaf,
Uncovering both joy and grief.
Through cluttered pasts, we feel the weight,
Of wisdom lost, yet still innate.

In this embrace of soft decay,
Grace lingers on in quiet sway.
Among the tomes, our hearts intertwine,
In dusty grace, a love divine.

The Rhythm of Obscured Truths

In shadows deep, the rhythm flows,
Obscured truths in silence grow.
A beat that thrums beneath the skin,
Where darkened paths begin to spin.

Each thought a wave, a silent tide,
That speaks of fears we try to hide.
In hidden beats of time and space,
The heart reveals a forgotten place.

Through tangled webs of night we chase,
The whispered echoes of our grace.
In moments lost to fleeting sight,
We find our path back to the light.

The rhythm guides, it never sleeps,
In depths where quiet knowledge keeps.
Embrace the truths, albeit obscure,
For in their depths, our souls endure.

Ode to the Isolated Archives

In dusty halls where echoes sleep,
Old tomes reveal the secrets they keep.
Pages yellowed by time's gentle hand,
Silent stories from a distant land.

Whispers linger in the musty air,
Ghosts of thoughts, both profound and rare.
Each spine a vessel, each word a key,
Unlocking worlds that long to be free.

Here moss-covered histories unfold,
Memories written and gently told.
A haven for those who seek and find,
The treasures of a curious mind.

In this refuge where few dare to tread,
Conversations linger even when dead.
It's here, within these walls, we strive,
To keep the past and present alive.

Poetic Whispers of the Shadows

In twilight's grasp, the shadows sway,
A silent dance at the end of day.
Whispers glide on the evening breeze,
Carrying secrets among the trees.

Softly spoken, like fragile dreams,
Drifting through the moonlit beams.
They weave a fabric of night's embrace,
Inviting us into their hidden space.

With every sigh, a tale unfolds,
Of long-lost hopes and futures bold.
In the stillness, we listen close,
To the quiet voice that beckons most.

These poetic murmurs draw us near,
A chorus of what we long to hear.
In the shadows, we find our lore,
And leave behind what was before.

Curated Thoughts in Secluded Places

Nestled deep in a quiet glade,
Curated thoughts in silence laid.
Beneath the boughs where sunlight fades,
A world of wonder serenely wades.

Each whispered breeze carries a clue,
To dreams pursued and visions true.
In solitude, creativity grows,
A tapestry of what one knows.

With every rustling leaf a sigh,
Thoughts ascend and freely fly.
Here, where distractions fade away,
Imagination finds its play.

In corners hidden from the light,
Ideas blossom out of sight.
In these sanctuaries, we explore,
Curated thoughts forevermore.

Lyrics Amidst the Stonework

Amidst the stonework, voices rise,
Carved in echoes of ancient sighs.
Each chiseled verse, a heartfelt plea,
Whispers of lives that used to be.

Abandoned halls and crumbling walls,
Resonate with their lonely calls.
Lyrics entwined with dust and grime,
Capturing moments lost in time.

With every crack, a story wakes,
Through fractured dreams and timeless aches.
In the shadows, the past demands,
A memory glimmers through forgotten lands.

Here, stone and spirit intertwine,
A reminder of the design.
In silent songs, we find our place,
Lyrics reveal a warm embrace.

Whispers of the Hidden Chamber

In the shadows, secrets lie,
Softly spoken, a gentle sigh.
Walls that hush, a silent plea,
Echoes drift, enticing me.

Mysteries wrapped in twilight's embrace,
Flickering lights in a hidden place.
Ancient tales of love and fear,
Whispers linger, always near.

Curious souls dare to explore,
Unlocking truths of times before.
The hidden chamber holds its breath,
Guarding stories of life and death.

With every step, the past unfolds,
A tapestry of dreams retold.
In this magic, shadows gleam,
Lost in time, we dare to dream.

Secrets Beneath the Stone

Deep beneath the ancient stone,
Lies a world we've never known.
Echoes of ages lost in sleep,
Buried secrets, piled deep.

Whispers ride the evening breeze,
Carried through the rustling leaves.
Every crack, a tale to tell,
Of forgotten joys and farewells.

In the twilight, shadows creep,
Guardians of the dreams we keep.
A glimmer here, a spark of light,
Guiding hearts through the endless night.

With hands that touch and eyes that see,
We uncover what's yet to be.
In the silence, answers flow,
Secrets beneath the stone will grow.

Echoes in the Forgotten Hall

Echoes linger, faint and frail,
In the hall where dreams set sail.
Whispers of laughter, shadows play,
Time stands still at end of day.

Forgotten stories, dust enshrined,
Fragments of a golden mind.
Every step a memory calls,
In the depth of these old walls.

Light dances softly on the floor,
Highlighting what was there before.
Glimmers of love, hope, and strife,
Resounding through the pulse of life.

In the stillness, we can find,
The echoes of a world once kind.
In forgotten halls, we trace the past,
Unraveling shadows, holding fast.

The Library of Lost Dreams

In the library, dreams reside,
Tucked in corners, nowhere to hide.
Silent pages, stories untold,
Treasures hidden, waiting to unfold.

The scent of parchment, old and wise,
Tells of journeys beneath new skies.
Faded ink, a glimpse of fate,
Yearning hearts anticipate.

Books that gather dust and time,
Hold the beauty of the sublime.
Each spine whispers of what could be,
A world alive with mystery.

In the hush, imagination roams,
Finding solace, building homes.
From the whispers, dreams ignite,
In the library, hearts take flight.

Inscriptions from the Depths

Etched in stone, the stories lie,
Whispers of time in silence sigh.
Roots entwined, through shadows creep,
Secrets buried, the earth will keep.

In the dark, the echoes call,
History waits behind the wall.
Footsteps fade on ancient trails,
Life's forgotten, where time prevails.

Tales of old in dim-lit caves,
Lost to light, the yearning saves.
Words of wisdom, carved through years,
Elusive truths, concealed in fears.

Amidst the stones, the past retains,
Lives entwined in whispered chains.
Inscriptions deep, we seek to find,
The soul's reflection, intertwined.

The Grotto of Silent Thoughts

In the grotto where shadows fall,
Echoes linger, a muted call.
Reflections dance on waters clear,
Thoughts submerged, but ever near.

Light and dark, they intertwine,
Fleeting hopes like rising wine.
A fortress made of silence grows,
Beneath the surface, wisdom flows.

Hidden dreams in caverned halls,
Gentle whispers, the heart enthralls.
Each breath a story, softly spun,
In quiet depths, where all begun.

In the still, where silence speaks,
The deepest truth the heart now seeks.
Glimmers fade, yet always yearn,
For the light, to which we turn.

Forgotten Fables in the Dark

In the dark, where fables sleep,
Whispers weave and shadows creep.
Stories lost to time's embrace,
Yet their echoes leave a trace.

Woven tales of yesteryear,
Carried forth through ghostly cheer.
Legends whisper on the breeze,
Beneath the trees, with rustling leaves.

Flickering flames bring life anew,
Inspiring hearts to seek the true.
A dance of light, a spark of thought,
Forgotten fables, now are sought.

Through the dark, the tales will guide,
With every word, dreams coincide.
In memory's vault, they seek to roam,
The heart's dwellings—their eternal home.

Loopholes in the Fabric of Memory

In memory's weave, threads are lost,
Where moments fade, and meanings cost.
Fragile patterns, delicate marks,
Time's swift dance leaves hidden sparks.

Glimmers of joy, shadows of pain,
Through loopholes, we chart the gain.
Fragments linger, we piece them right,
A tapestry of day and night.

Thoughts like rivers twisting bend,
Through ages, they curve and blend.
In the fabric, truth might fray,
Yet remnants linger, come what may.

A kaleidoscope of faces seen,
In depths of mind where dreams have been.
Through every loop, we seek to mend,
The threads of time that do not end.

Unraveled Tales in Enclosed Spaces

In corners dark where whispers creep,
Secrets linger, shadows leap.
Walls confide in hushed tones low,
Revealing tales the world won't know.

Beneath the dust, old stories sigh,
Of laughter, joy, a bittersweet lie.
Forgotten dreams in silence freeze,
In cloistered rooms, the heart's unease.

A tapestry of lives entwined,
Fragments lost, yet still confined.
Each crack a voice, each mark a clue,
In hidden realms, where trust once grew.

To wander through these cherished halls,
Is to embrace what time recalls.
In every nook, a lesson dwells,
In enclosed spaces, unraveling spells.

Subdued Echoes of the Enigma

Beneath the stars, the silence holds,
A tapestry of secrets enfolds.
Echoes murmur in the night air,
Telling tales of dreams laid bare.

In the shadows, whispers dance,
A fleeting truth, a fleeting chance.
The heart beats with a rhythm strange,
In the enigma, lives rearrange.

Hushed confessions ride the breeze,
A subtle brush of mystery's tease.
Each passing moment breathes a sigh,
Subdued echoes, as time slips by.

To ponder what the silence keeps,
In deep reflections, the mystery sleeps.
With every breath, a question posed,
In the quiet, the enigma grows.

Mysteries Written In Time

In sands of time, the stories lie,
Fragments of dreams that dared to fly.
Each grain a whisper, lost in flow,
Mysteries written, for time to know.

Beneath the stars, where shadows blend,
The paper trails of lives transcend.
Ink spills secrets, yearning to rhyme,
In every stroke, a pulse of time.

Chronicles of love and strife,
Etched in the fabric of life.
Each moment captured, bound in place,
Mysteries held in time's embrace.

To wander through this shifting maze,
Is to uncover lost yesterdays.
In gentle hues, the stories gleam,
Mysteries woven in history's dream.

The Sonnet of Stalwart Stones

Upon the hill, the stones stand proud,
Guardians silent, beneath the cloud.
Ancient tales in their silence speak,
Of battles won and futures bleak.

With weathered faces, they tell the tale,
Of tempest winds and whispered wail.
In every crack, a history flows,
The sonnet sung where the wild rose grows.

Together bound in timeless grace,
Each stone a shadow, a lingering trace.
In unity, the strength they show,
Through seasons' change, they ebb and flow.

To walk among these stalwart forms,
Is to feel the pulse of ancient storms.
In every stone, a world to find,
A sonnet etched for the curious mind.

The Poetry Within the Walls

Whispers dance in silent halls,
Echoes of life, the past recalls.
Ink stains from thoughts once unfurled,
Stories long lost to another world.

Beneath the surface, the shadows play,
Words linger softly, night and day.
Secrets woven in each creak and bend,
Time stands still; it won't pretend.

Every brick holds a voice profound,
Melodies forgotten, barely found.
In corners shrouded, musings wait,
In the stillness, they resonate.

The heart of ages beats in stone,
In every fracture, wisdom grown.
Listening close, the silence thrums,
In the walls, a heartbeat hums.

Elusive Expressions of the Past

Fleeting glances caught in time,
Softly spoken, a whispered rhyme.
Fragments scatter on the breeze,
Echoes hide among the trees.

Brush of colors, once so bright,
Memories dimmed in fading light.
Captured moments, lost in haze,
Yearning for those golden days.

Each shadow casts a dreamer's sigh,
Unraveled tales of days gone by.
Captured laughter, now turned gray,
In silent whispers, they drift away.

Fingers trace the lines of time,
In verses written, stories climb.
Elusive treasures, forever sought,
In every heartbeat, we are caught.

The Song of Sealed Memories

Hushed and quiet, secrets lie,
Bottled laughter, a muted cry.
Gentle echoes wrap the air,
In the silence, memories bear.

Tread softly where the shadows creep,
In stillness, unspoken vows keep.
Each sealed moment, a hidden tune,
In twilight's glow, they softly croon.

Threads of time weave a soft refrain,
Notes of joy, whispers of pain.
Underneath the surface, they flow,
In the heart, their stories grow.

Unlock the melodies buried deep,
In the quiet, their secrets seep.
Listen closely; let them sing,
In sealed memories, the heart takes wing.

Hidden Lullabies in Twilight

As dusk descends, the world grows still,
Crickets serenade, the night's sweet thrill.
Moonlight dances on waters clear,
In gentle whispers, dreams draw near.

Veils of twilight, soft and light,
Cradle secrets in the night.
Hushed lullabies drift on the breeze,
Nature's chorus puts the soul at ease.

Stars awaken, a twinkling choir,
Songs of longing, hearts conspire.
Each note woven with tender care,
Hidden lullabies linger in the air.

In the stillness, peace unfurls,
A tapestry of dreams whirls.
Embrace the calm, let the world sway,
In hidden lullabies, find your way.

Echoing Sonatas from the Depths

In caverns deep where whispers dwell,
Echoes rise like a secret spell.
Notes of sorrow, tales of old,
In shadows sung, a world unfolds.

Fingers dance on strings of night,
Casting dreams in silver light.
Melodies lost in the vast abyss,
Calling forth a haunting bliss.

The river flows, a timeless sigh,
While moonlight weaves through the sky.
Each sound a memory, softly cast,
Echoing sonatas from the past.

In every note, a heartbeat beats,
Resonance where the darkness meets.
A symphony of phantom grace,
In tangled depths, we find our place.

The Spirit of Lost Manuscripts

In dusty halls where shadows creep,
The echoes of lost tales sleep.
Ink-stained pages whisper low,
Secrets written long ago.

A faded quill, a poet's hand,
Crafting worlds, both vast and grand.
Ghostly figures in the night,
Searching for the lost light.

Time-stamped words on crumbling leaves,
A tapestry of forgotten dreams.
The spirit stirs, begins to rise,
To weave again with silver ties.

With every stroke, the past appears,
Mending gaps with silent tears.
The manuscripts speak soft and clear,
Of voices lost, yet ever near.

Chords of the Obscured

In twilight's grasp, where shadows play,
Chords arise from the depths of gray.
Harmony hangs in the misty air,
Singing songs of a world laid bare.

Strings do tremble, a fragile thread,
Binding hearts to what was said.
Whispers linger on the breeze,
Echoing through the ancient trees.

Forgotten tales in the dark unwind,
Labyrinths of the lost entwined.
Notes escape in a gentle flow,
Guiding souls through ebb and flow.

In this dusk, the music calls,
Awakening visions behind the walls.
Chords of the obscured unite,
A tapestry woven in the night.

Echoes of an Ancient Lament

The wind carries a mournful tune,
Beneath the gaze of the pale moon.
Whispers rise from forgotten graves,
Echoes of what the heart still craves.

Silent cries in the still of night,
A fading dream, lost to the light.
With every sigh, a story breaks,
Of love once held, and how it aches.

Songbirds hush, as shadows creep,
Vows once made, now silence keeps.
In the garden where memories bloom,
An ancient lament fills the room.

Each note drips with the weight of years,
A symphony of sorrow appears.
Together sung, though worlds apart,
Echoes linger within the heart.